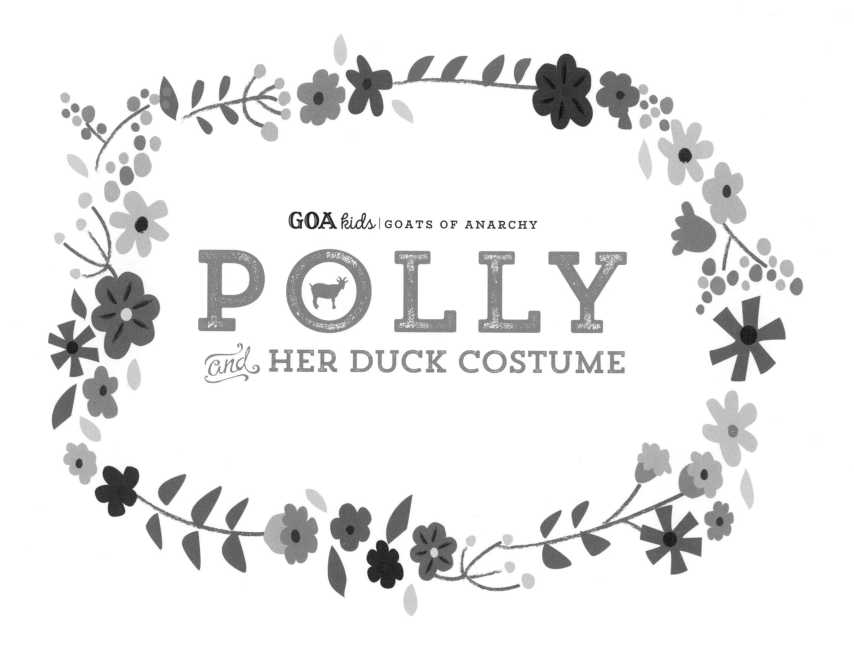

GOA *kids* | GOATS OF ANARCHY

POLLY

and HER DUCK COSTUME

Brimming with creative inspiration, how-to projects, and useful information to enrich your everyday life, Quarto Knows is a favorite destination for those pursuing their interests and passions. Visit our site and dig deeper with our books into your area of interest: Quarto Creates, Quarto Cooks, Quarto Homes, Quarto Lives,

© 2017 Quarto Publishing Group USA Inc.
Text © Leanne Lauricella

First Published in 2017 by Walter Foster Jr., an imprint of The Quarto Group.
6 Orchard Road, Suite 100, Lake Forest, CA 92630, USA.
T (949) 380-7510 F (949) 380-7575 **www.QuartoKnows.com**

Walter Foster Publishing titles are also available at discount for retail, wholesale, promotional, and bulk purchase. For details, contact the Special Sales Manager by email at specialsales@quarto.com or by mail at The Quarto Group, Attn: Special Sales Manager, 401 Second Avenue North, Suite 310, Minneapolis, MN 55401 USA.

ISBN: 978-1-63322-418-6

Digital edition published in 2017
eISBN: 978-1-63322-419-3

Content development by Saskia Lacey
Illustrated by Jill Howarth

Printed in China
10 9 8 7 6 5 4 3 2 1

GOA *kids* | GOATS OF ANARCHY

POLLY

and HER DUCK COSTUME

By **LEANNE LAURICELLA** with *Saskia Lacey*

Illustrated by **JILL HOWARTH**

Polly was different from the start. She could hear the birds sing and smell the crisp, spring air. But she could not see the blue sky or its clouds. Polly was blind.

More than anything, Polly longed to be loved. She sometimes went hungry, and was very lonely.

Polly only felt warm and safe
when she nestled deep in the hay.

One day, a young woman came to the farm and cradled the goat in her arms. "Don't worry," she said. "You're coming home with me. Everything will be okay now."

Polly's new mom brought her home, wrapped her in a blanket, and cuddled her close. With a small huff, Polly fell right to sleep.

G.O.A.

Every day, Polly's mom took her on walks through the house, helping the little goat learn the shape of each room.

Polly perked up her ears, listening carefully. She followed the sound of her mom's voice.

When she was hungry, Polly waddled happily to the kitchen. Before drinking from her bottle, she always gave a little snort, just like a piglet!

But Polly's favorite thing to do was snuggle on the couch, wrapped tightly in a blanket.

One morning, Polly's mom went outside to feed the other animals. When Polly woke, she called for her mom, but the house was quiet.

Polly grew anxious. She checked each room in the house, but no one was there.

She stamped her hoof. She called out, "Mama!"

But no one answered.

"Where's my mom?" wondered Polly.
She hid in a corner, too scared to move.

When her mom came back inside, she picked Polly up
and bundled her in a blanket to comfort her. Warm
and safe, Polly breathed easy again.

Polly always felt best when she was wrapped in a blanket. But as soon as she stood up, she would lose her blanket! Polly's mom knew she needed something different.

One day, she picked Polly up and wrapped her in something new— it was warm and fuzzy and so comfortable!

Polly curled up on the couch and soon fell fast asleep.

Polly adored her new fuzzy coat.
She wore it *everywhere,* even to the store.

As she rode in a shopping cart, she heard all the
people say, "Look at that goat dressed like a duck!"
Some gasped and some giggled with delight.

Polly had never seen a duck, but she didn't mind.
All that mattered was that Polly felt safe and happy.

When Polly was wearing her duck costume,
she didn't worry about a single thing, and all
was right in the world.

One day while happily snoozing, Polly felt a tickle at her ear.

What could it be?

She sniffed the air and felt around with her nose. There was a tiny baby goat beside her!

Her name was Pippa, and she was a rescue goat too. She had hurt her legs, and she wore bandages to help them heal.

Polly and Pippa quickly became friends.
The tiny goat followed Polly wherever she went.

Polly soon outgrew her duck costume, but it was a perfect fit for Pippa!

Polly's mom found a new duck costume that fit Polly just right.

Polly and Pippa did everything together, and never strayed more than a tail's length away.

Polly started to feel like the duck costume was getting in the way of playing with Pippa.

She decided to take it off, but just for a minute.

As time passed, Polly and Pippa became best friends. Hoof to hoof, the two little goats whispered and laughed and snuggled.

One day, Polly and Pippa's mom decided to take them to the store. She was about to put on Polly's duck costume, but she stopped.

Polly was busy playing with Pippa! Polly didn't need her duck costume anymore.

She had her mom, and Pippa, and a warm, happy place to call home.

The End

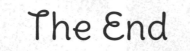

POLLY
and HER
DUCK COSTUME
The True Story

Hi, I'm Leanne Lauricella. People also call me "Goat Mama" because I rescue baby goats. I have a farm called *Goats of Anarchy* in New Jersey, where I care for more than 50 goats. Plus, we also take care of 2 lambs, 2 pigs, 6 dogs, chickens, and a miniature horse and miniature donkey. We have a very full house!

Leanne

Polly

This is the real Polly. When I first saw her, she was circling her small area at the farm. She was blind, and very small, and she was very anxious and scared. I fell in love with her right then and there and I brought her home with me.

Polly is unique. She only weighs about 25 pounds. That's less than half the weight of other goats her age!

Polly has a different kind of brain. It's what makes her blind but also what makes her special. When she was a baby, she liked to sit up straight on the couch like a person.

Polly's favorite costume

I originally bought the duck costume for Polly for Halloween. I thought it would be cute to dress her up! But from the first moment she put it on, the duck costume calmed her down completely. She wasn't the least bit scared or anxious anymore! In fact, she would often fall right to sleep.

Polly grew out of the original costume I bought her, so she gave it to little Pippa and it fit perfectly. Polly got a new duck costume that fit her just right, and now she and Pippa can both be ducks together!

These days, Polly hardly ever gets anxious anymore, but she loves to take naps on the couch and eat her favorite meal: pumpkin carrot baby food. She also loves to snuggle with her new friend, Pepper, a partially blind baby goat that just joined the family!

Pepper and Polly

Polly and her friend Pocket

Pippa and Polly

Polly is a star!

♥ Sweet Polly